Everything You Need to Know
*about* Garage & Yard Sales

# Everything You Need to Know *about* Garage & Yard Sales

### Be Better Organized, Have Fun, and Sell More

## JON FULGHUM

iUniverse, Inc.
New York  Lincoln  Shanghai

**Everything You Need to Know
about Garage & Yard Sales
Be Better Organized, Have Fun, and Sell More**

Copyright © 2007 by Jon F. Fulghum

iUniverse books may be ordered through booksellers or
by contacting:

iUniverse
2021 Pine Lake Road, Suite 100
Lincoln, NE 68512
www.iuniverse.com
1-800-Authors (1-800-288-4677)

ISBN-13: 978-0-595-41744-5 (pbk)
ISBN-13: 978-0-595-86084-5 (ebk)
ISBN-10: 0-595-41744-2 (pbk)
ISBN-10: 0-595-86084-2 (ebk)

Printed in the United States of America

# CONTENTS

# ACKNOWLEDGMENT

This book would not have been possible had it not been for the person who first introduced me to the rewarding world of garage and yard sales—my friend, Gordon Mills. Gordon has been my mentor, as well as my garage and yard sale shopping guru on many outings. I have learned much from him regarding how sales should be organized and conducted in order to be successful.

Thank you, Gordon!

# INTRODUCTION

Garage and yard sales have become regular events in our society. Each year, thousands of such sales totaling millions of dollars take place.

Many people don't recognize the economic benefit these sales provide us. They are effective tools for the redistribution of goods that might not otherwise be fully utilized. Also, they have value from a standard-of-living point of view. The prices of garage and yard sale items allow shoppers to satisfy various needs or desires and still have money to spare for other things. Lastly, the money earned by those who conduct such sales is ultimately exchanged for other goods and services, as opposed to being tied up in items that are not being used and/or just being stored.

These sales function in a completely free market. They are neither regulated nor taxed. The success of each sale is determined by the negotiations that take place during the sale. It is too bad then that most such sales are not as successful as they could be.

The purpose of this book is to share the secrets of conducting a successful garage or yard sale.

As you read this book you might notice that the text makes no distinction between garage sales and yard sales. This is purposeful. Weather aside, for the most part garage sales spill out into the driveway, and yard sales encroach on garage and driveway space. Thus the preference for the use of one name over the other is more a result of customary community usage rather than anything of substance. Therefore, for convenience throughout the remainder of this book, these sales will be generally referred to simply as garage sales.

It is interesting to note that some communities use alternative names and locations for garage sales. In some parts of the country, names such as carport sales, sidewalk sales, personal-property sales, tag sales, and stoop sales will be used. In any case, the text of this book applies to whatever you wish to call these sales and wherever you wish to conduct them. This is what makes this book unique!

Lastly, the "how to" information in this book is practical, enlightening, and easy to apply. What you will learn from it will enable you to effectively organize truly successful garage sales.

# CHAPTER ONE

# WHY A GARAGE OR YARD SALE?

This question might seem unnecessary to anyone who has opened this book. However, since there are a number of reasons for conducting these sales and each usually requires somewhat different planning, formulating a clear answer to this question now will ultimately be very helpful to you.

Basically, these sales are conducted to achieve one or more of the following purposes:

- ✓ To get rid of things that you no longer want or find useful
- ✓ To downsize possessions
- ✓ To prepare for a relocation
- ✓ To dispose of part or all of the remains of an estate
- ✓ To make money for personal use
- ✓ To earn money for charity

Regardless of purpose, the underlying objective of each of the above will always be to dispose of unwanted goods in the hope of earning a few dollars while doing so.

Of course, there are several ways to dispose of unwanted goods. For example, you could throw them away, which would enable you to immediately get rid of them. You could also give them to charity. However, the choice between these options tends to bring to mind the conservation issue that is the fundamental premise for all recycling; we should not be destroying things that can in some way be useful to or used again by others.

If you value recycling, but would still like to make a few dollars in the process, then the garage sale option is the right thing for you. On the other hand, if you don't think that the efforts required to conduct a sale will be worth the dollars to be made, at least give your unwanted items to charity or find some other way to recycle them. In any case in your deliberation, it is crucial that you understand that recycled goods will never bring the prices that were paid for them when they were new, no matter how valuable or useful they have been to you in the past.

If, so far, you are still interested in considering a garage sale, there are a few more questions that you should ask yourself:

1. Can I become fully committed to sell all of the items that I include in the sale?
2. Can I be flexible in my asking price?
3. Can I devote the time it will take to plan and carry out a successful sale?

Let's examine each of these questions.

## Fully Committed to Sell or Not

If you are going to conduct a successful garage sale, you must be fully committed from the beginning to giving up the items offered, without reservations and without concerns about their intended use. If you can't bear to part with certain items, don't offer them for sale! If you do, you will be hurting yourself and stifling the results of your sale.

There are some people who even after thoughtfully selecting items they are willing to sell ultimately experience twinges of remorse about giving them up. For one reason or another, during their sale they suddenly seem to develop a renewed sense of attachment to certain items and almost defy anyone who shows the slightest interest in buying them. They seem to take the sale of such items personally both in terms of price and prospective use. The price becomes nonnegotiable, and their response to a proposed use can turn to hostility, even to the extent of refusing to sell the item to an "undeserving" buyer.

A good example of this phenomena might be the sale of a quilt that was handmade by a departed family member. When a potential buyer remarks that it would be a good dog blanket, the seller might become offended and refuse to sell it to "someone who is so insensitive."

## Flexibility in the Asking Price

Of all the things that can diminish the success of your sale being inflexible on price is the greatest.

Being flexible on price takes two forms: (1) initially setting a price that seems generally fair and (2) being willing to negotiate a somewhat lower price. Always remember the objective of any garage sale is to get rid of items—not keep them. Pricing an item at $7.00 that you paid $30 for ten years ago and ultimately selling it for $5.00 is better than holding on to it forever. Getting rid of unwanted and unneeded items plus being compensated to some degree for your efforts is far better than allowing them to take up space in your home for years to come.

## Willingness to Devote the Time to Have a Successful Sale

To have a successful sale, you must be willing to do some planning and a little physical work. In preparation for the sale, you will need to plan and accomplish the following tasks:

1. Familiarize yourself with local ordnances, if any, that might impact the conduct of your sale.

2. Locate all the items that you wish to offer for sale by searching through your entire house, garage, storage shed, etc.

3. Assemble the sale items in one place such as a garage, carport, spare bedroom, closet, etc.

4. Inventory and clearly mark a price on each item or bundle of items.

5. Call the local newspaper and any other widely read publication with a classified section and place

an order for an advertisement for the sale date or dates.

6. Prepare neighborhood signs to direct potential buyers to the sale location.

7. Secure enough money, bills as well as coins, to minimize problems making correct change.

8. Display the items being offered in an orderly fashion and in an area that is clean, well illuminated, free of unpleasant odors, and otherwise free of visual distractions.

9. Accumulate a supply of boxes and/or bags so buyers will have containers in which to carry their purchases.

10. Arrange to park your family's vehicles at a neighbor's house or in parking spaces out of the way of the sale.

11. Set up a checkout stand or table at the most likely exit point or in the most clearly visible area.

12. Provide soft background music that will encourage a relaxed and inviting atmosphere.

13. Ask spouse, friends, relatives, etc. to assist during the sale by welcoming potential buyers, keeping track of the items being offered and/or sold, assisting

with questions, and providing you with relief when needed.

14. Notify all of your immediate neighbors of the upcoming sale so that they can block off their driveways or parking spaces to keep them clear if this is an issue.

If you can't envision yourself planning and accomplishing the above to have a successful sale, forget the sale and have everything picked up by a charity or hauled away in the trash. A half-hearted effort will almost always lead to disappointing results, which is something you probably don't need.

# CHAPTER TWO

# TYPES OF GARAGE OR YARD SALES

There are six basic types of sales you should know about:

- Single family
- Multi-family
- Community
- Estate
- Charity
- Rummage

Single family sales are the most common. You have this kind of sale when your family decides to sell a number of items that you no longer need and the number and type of items are sufficient to make it attractive to prospective shoppers. If your family does not have many items, you should consider combining your items with those of other families and organizing a multi-family sale.

Multi-family sales are made up of the items from two or more different families that are assembled for sale in one location. Because multi-family sales tend to be larger than single-family sales, you can usually attract more potential buyers to a multi-family sale; however, it is sometimes complicated to keep track of the sales that belong to each family.

Community sales are events in which a number of different families in a defined geographical area agree to simultaneously conduct individual sales. Your homeowners association, social club, or apartment complex, etc. may decide to organize one of these events. Because these sales have the potential to be very large and usually attract many shoppers, it is a good idea to participate in one of these when you have the opportunity. It is often easier to sell your own items in a community sale than to cooperate with several families in coordinating a multi-family sale.

Estate sales are non-auction sales that include everything, or a significant number of items, from someone's estate. You would have one of these sales after a death in the family, a decision to downsize significantly or a commitment is made to a major relocation. Although you might consider personally handling such a sale, they are usually organized, for a percentage of the sales, by people who do so for a living. In estate sales everything offered will be sold! The organizers are usually firm on the marked prices for the first day and then deeply discount them on the second and subsequent days. At the end of the sale, they generally sell any remaining items as an entire lot to a professional consolidator. When it comes to estate sales, many people believe that non-auction sales are more cost effective than traditional auctions. You will find this is particularly true when the number of sale items is somewhat modest and the estate does not include a significant number of valuable antiques and/or collectibles.

Charity sales are ones in which you, along with any number of other people, contribute items to be sold by others. The organizers assume the responsibility for collecting these items and conducting the sales at one or more individual neighborhood locations. The dollar proceeds of the sales are then donated to a preferred charity or some entity with special needs. Some people have a tendency to call these sales rummage sales, but this is not quite accurate. Charity sales are simply the work of a few motivated individuals and are usually not directly sponsored by any of the charities or entities that might benefit from their proceeds.

Rummage sales are like charity sales in that their organizers collect sale items from different people and take the responsibility for selling them. However, they are not like charity sales in that they generally have a direct sponsorship relationship with a church or other notable charitable organization that will be the sole beneficiary of their sales' results. Additionally, in most cases rummage sales are held on the premises of the sponsoring entity as opposed to one or more individual neighborhood locations.

# CHAPTER THREE

## WHEN TO HAVE A GARAGE OR YARD SALE

Because garage sales are traditionally open-air events, the climate and weather have much to do with the number of shoppers who will show up for your sale. If it is freezing, snowing, or storming, you cannot expect a significant turnout.

In most parts of the United States, the best time to conduct these sales is from the beginning of spring through early fall. However, if you live in a temperate area and your winter months are moderate, you can successfully plan your sales almost any time.

Unfortunately, no matter where you live, inclement weather is occasionally an issue. If such weather appears eminent, consider changing the date or dates for your sale. No one is going to be excited about buying weathered items on a dreary day in gale-force winds. If rescheduling becomes necessary, quickly amend all of your previous advertising and promotional efforts. You will need to be prompt in getting the word out about the change. If you have already posted notices or signs, attach banners to them announcing the cancellation and rescheduled date or dates, plus any other information that needs updating. Rescheduling does not mean that your sale is a disaster. It simply means that for the benefit of all concerned you have selected a better time to conduct your sale.

Friday, Saturday, and Sunday are the best days for your sale. Saturday and Sunday are traditional shopping days for most people, and with the growing number of retirees and people who do not like to shop on the weekend, Fridays can also be very good sale days.

The best hours to conduct a sale are usually from 7:00 AM to 5:00 PM. These hours will generally accommodate most potential buyers, including those who have flexible work schedules or simply wish to shop early or late in a day.

# CHAPTER FOUR

# TYPES OF SHOPPERS

There are five basic types of shoppers you should know about:

- Merchants
- Collectors
- Hunters
- Opportunists
- Missionaries

Merchants are people who look for specific items that they can use and/or resell in their established businesses. They will generally be among the first wave of potential buyers at your sale, and, if at all possible, they will try to examine all of your sale items before your sale is scheduled to start. Shoppers such as these who tend to arrive early are generally referred to as "early-birds." If you have advertised an 8:00 AM start time, they may show up as much as an hour before.

They are looking to purchase the best of what you are offering for their businesses.

Collectors are usually individuals who are looking for items to add to one or more of their personal collections. They, too, are often early-bird shoppers. However, unlike merchants, whose search is more focused, collectors are not opposed to picking up a wider range of items.

Hunters are people who simply like going to garage sales on a regular basis. In some cases they make a habit of going to as many sales as possible as often as possible in hopes of finding things they like or can use at a good price. For these people it is the "thrill of the hunt" that motivates them.

Opportunists are people who are attracted by an advertisement, direction sign, sale location, etc., and respond by taking a few unplanned minutes to stop at a sale and examine the sale's items. These people may have never gone to a garage sale before, and it may be some time before they go to another one. However, for some reason, they feel compelled to visit a particular sale.

Missionaries are people who generally work directly with a church group or other charity. They shop at garage sales to buy low-cost items that are needed by the less fortunate.

These potential buyers typically look for items such as clothes, kitchen supplies, children's toys, etc. Although missionaries will not represent a large segment of shoppers or potential buyers, the number of items that they buy and their dollar purchases can be significant.

# CHAPTER FIVE

# WHAT SHOPPERS LOOK FOR

Most of the shoppers at your garage sale will generally buy on an impulse basis. Unless they are merchants, collectors, or missionaries they will not usually come with a shopping list. However, regardless of the type shopper most will still be willing to purchase items they had not previously considered if what they find will serve a useful purpose.

Garage sale shoppers are generally looking for two major things: value and price—in that order.

Shoppers will only buy the items in your sale if they believe that what they are buying is both useful and desirable—has value to them. You can offer a silver tea set for only $50, but if none of the shoppers who attend your sale see the tea set as useful and desirable, it will not sell no matter how attractive you believe your price to be. Fortunately for you, different shoppers usually have different perceptions of the value of the same item.

As for price, most potential buyers are looking for "a great deal." A great deal is a price that is both attractive and easily affordable. It is usually thought of as one that is beyond good. Most people who attend garage sales have no interest in paying even discount-store prices. They are only interested in buying items for really low prices and walking away feeling that they got "a great deal." This is what they believe these sales are all about!

# CHAPTER SIX

## WHAT ITEMS TO OFFER

In essence, there are no real limitations on the items that can be offered for sale at garage sales. However, careful consideration should be given to offering high-priced items like automobiles, tractors, expensive jewelry, etc. If you have a need to include such items, you should advertise them separately with detailed descriptions and asking prices. Unless specifically advertised, people who attend garage sales typically do not come prepared to consider the purchase of high-priced items.

You should also consider not offering personal hygiene items, over-the-counter medications, and adult entertainment items. Offering these types of items is generally viewed as being in poor taste.

It is not uncommon to offer clothes that these sale. However, if you choose to do so the clothes that you offer should be clean, be in reasonably good condition, have sizes clearly marked, and be displayed effectively. Piles of stained or tattered clothing on an oil-spotted, dirty garage floor or driveway will attract few buyers and do nothing to encourage shoppers to spend more time examining the other items that you have for sale.

No doubt as you select items for your sale you will discover items that are not in good condition and do not have much life left in them. If you decide that they are not worth selling but you still feel they could be of value to someone, consider putting these items in a "Free" box. Usually a Free box is simply a cardboard box with a sign on the front that says FREE. At the end of the sale, if there are any items left in the Free box, give them to charity, or throw them away.

# CHAPTER SEVEN

# CONSIGNMENT ITEMS

As word of your sale spreads, you may find that there are people who do not want to have any part in organizing or conducting your sale but who do have items they would like you to sell for them.

If you feel that the items they wish to include in your sale will make it more attractive to shoppers, consider accepting these items on a consignment basis. However, since this is your sale and you will be doing all of the work to promote it, you should also consider charging any consignor a selling fee, such as 10 percent of the final sale price of each item. You should settle this issue before accepting any consignment items.

Additionally, because potential buyers of consignment items may wish to negotiate final prices and the consignors may not be immediately accessible, you should have a minimum sale-price agreement for each item. If you do not, there is a good possibility you could sell an item or items for less than expected, which could cause a lot of ill will.

Finally, some consignors have a tendency to be lax when it comes to picking up unsold items. You should make sure they have agreed to a deadline for picking up such items before you agree to accept them.

# CHAPTER EIGHT

# ADVERTISING AND PROMOTION

The purpose of advertising and promotion is to get the word out regarding your sale and direct people to its location. You can have a sale, but if only a few close neighbors know about it, it will have little chance of being successful.

Some great advertising methods include:

- Advertising in the classified section of a local newspaper and/or shoppers' publication
- Distributing announcement flyers
- Making brief announcements during club or organization meetings
- Posting announcements on community bulletin boards
- Preparing and positioning signs to attract and direct shoppers to the sale location

## Advertising

Prior to the actual sale date or dates, you should contact your local newspaper and/or shoppers' news publication and place an announcement of your sale in their classified sections.

At minimum, your announcement should include: (1) the date or dates of the sale; (2) the hours of the sale; (3) the address and directions to the sale, if difficult to locate; (4) a brief list of some of the "highlight" items that will be included in the sale (i.e., electronics, coin collections, antique furniture, cook books, baby clothes, power tools, etc.); and (5) the type of sale if other than a single-family sale, e.g., community, multifamily, estate, charity or rummage sale.

There are several other things that you might consider including in your ad. For instance, if your sales will be "cash only" or if early birds will not be allowed, this can be noted. (Remember, early birds are any shoppers who want to begin examining the sale items just before the sale is scheduled to start. This is usually considered unfair to the other shoppers who respect your start time.) Also, you might like to begin your ad with bold phrases like: "Large Sale," "House-Clearing Sale," "Moving Sale," "Real Yard Sale," "Everything Sale,"

"Unbelievable Sidewalk Sale," "Estate Sale," "Don't Miss Sale," "Rain Or Shine Sale," "Must-See Sale," etc. You might also choose to place dark borders around your ad so that it will stand out from adjacent ads. Obviously there are numerous things that you can do to highlight your advertisements, but keep in mind that anything beyond the basics may not be cost effective. Garage-sale shoppers are usually familiar with such sales and will tend to look at all of the ads, regardless of your efforts to capture their attention.

Don't try to save money by not advertising until the day of the sale. Many shoppers like to plan their shopping excursions the day before the sales are scheduled to begin. This allows them to start early and get to most of the sales before the good items are gone. In fact, some people will begin their shopping excursions before receiving their morning paper. Thus, if you wait to advertise until the actual day of the sale, you will obviously miss a number of possible shoppers.

## Announcement Flyers

There are two basic types of sale announcement flyers: preliminary sale and sale promotion.

Preliminary sale announcement flyers are for organizing community sales. The organizers use them to notify all residents in their community of their intent to conduct a community sale and to solicit responses from those members of the community who want to participate. The received responses are then use to coordinate with those who wish to be involved.

Although you will mostly see preliminary announcement flyers during the organizational phase of community sales, you might also see them during the planning of multi-family sales. When used for multi-family sales, the main purpose is to encourage area neighbors to bring any items that they wish to sell to the single location where the planned sale is to be conducted.

The promotional flyers are used to announce the sale dates to the general public and encourage those who receive them to visit the sale. Promotional flyers will be effective for you if your sale will be held in a community with a high-density population. The compact nature of such communities makes flyer delivery easy and worthwhile. Since your sale will be close by, it will be very convenient for people who receive the flyer to come see what you are offering.

*Jon Fulghum*

Historically most garage sales are successfully conducted without going to the expense of creating and delivering promotional flyers. However, if you do not place an advertisement in a local newspaper or shoppers' news publication, you should seriously consider preparing and distributing flyers.

## Meeting Announcements

If you belong to a club or social organization, ask if you can briefly announce your upcoming sale during one of its meetings. You might discover that there are other members who would like to join with you and offer items for sale and/or volunteer to help you conduct your sale. This is one of those "no harm in trying" efforts. Plus, in the end you may generate more shoppers and potential buyers.

## Announcement Posting

Posting an announcement on a community bulletin board is a simple way to help advertise your upcoming sale. Just keep in mind that some organizations have very strict criteria for what can and cannot be posted on their bulletin boards. Obviously you would need to adhere to their criteria.

Also, when the sale is over, you should immediately remove your announcement. Not only is it the polite thing to do, but such timely action might make it easier for you to gain permission the next time you wish to post another announcement.

## Directional Signs

Poor directional signs will unquestionably reduce the success of your garage sale. Many times shoppers are unable to locate the sales that they are looking for because of poor directional signs. If people can't find your sale location, you have lost potential sales!

When it comes to directional signs, the following are "must do" items for single-family, multi-family, estate, charity, and rummage sales:

- Directional signs must be located in clear view from the closest major intersection to the actual sale location.
- Basic sign lettering must be bold and large.
- Each sign must use the same color material.
- Sign placement and anchoring must be consistent and effective.

## Sign Locations

Starting with the closest major intersection, place directional signs on every corner leading to the sale location. Also, if there are long distances between corners, you should place directional signs so that no matter how far someone has to travel to get to the sale, there is always a directional sign in sight.

## Sign Lettering

Print the words "garage sale," "yard sale," or whatever alternative sale name you are using in a dark, indelible color (to prevent running if exposed to moisture) with bold lettering at least two inches high. Add a directional arrow to the sign to correctly point the way to the sale. Draw the directional arrow in the same dark color as the lettering. It should be at least one inch wide.

If you want to, you could add your address to the sign in smaller letters just in case someone happens to get disoriented or lost and wishes to refer to a street map.

## Sign Consistency

Print the sign on stiff, light-colored material so that the dark lettering will stand out. However, as long as the lettering and arrow will be clearly visible, you could substitute a brighter colored material such as chartreuse or orange.

Make all of your signs out of the same material, and have the same color lettering. All your signs must be uniform so that shoppers will not get your signs confused with someone else's.

If you feel that drawing or painting signs is not one of your strengths, you can check with your local office supply, hardware, or discount store to find out if they have generic pre-printed sale signs that you can purchase. If they do, all you will be needed to do is to add arrows to point the way and print the address of your sale.

## Sign Placement & Anchoring

It is fair to assume that not all the property owners along the route to your sale are going to be willing to allow you to place and anchor your signs in their front yards. It is also possible that you might live in a neighborhood or community that does not allow such signs at all. Therefore, you should consider the following options:

- Attach the signs to the outside of cardboard boxes and place the cardboard boxes along the roads or sidewalks in your neighborhood. If you choose this option, it will be important to place rocks or other heavy objects inside the boxes to prevent the signs from blowing over or shifting in the wrong direction.

- If your sign material is flexible and can be folded, you may be able to create tent-type signs that you can place along roads and sidewalks and weight them down with rocks or other heavy material.

- You might be able to borrow metal real estate sign frames from a realtor. You can cover them with your signs and strategically place them along the route to your sale in much the same fashion as "open house" signs.

- You might also be able to attach your signs to wooden stakes and stick the stakes in the ground along the shoulders of the roads leading to your sale. The shoulders of roads are generally considered public property, and as long as your signs do not create a safety hazard or violate any ordinances you may be able to use these areas for your signs. (This location is one that many politicians favor when putting up their election campaign signs.) If you have trouble finding stakes, contact your local hardware or discount store for possible materials to use, including their wooden, five-gallon-paint-can stirring sticks that are usually free.

- If you live in an area where above-ground utility poles, street light standards, or street signposts are prevalent, you might be able to attach your signs to these structures for the brief duration of your sale.

- Assuming that your community or neighborhood permits on-street parking, you might also be able to temporarily park your friends' and family's vehicles at all the important intersections and place signs on the top or back of each vehicle.

- In the event that you live in a neighborhood or community that does not permit any signs, you could station one or more volunteers at the main entrance or entrances to your neighborhood or community with one large sign and a supply of location fliers that they can hand out to people who express an interest in the sale.

Community sales, which involve a number of different locations at one time, can take advantage of all of the above for advertising, announcement flyers, meeting announcements, and announcement posting. However, when it comes to directional signs, their needs will be different than those of single-family, multi-family, estate, charity, and rummage sales.

The following are "must do" directional sign items for community sales:

- Prepare large signs that note the dates and times of the sale and post them at each major entrance to the community.

- Place volunteers at each major entrance to hand out maps of the community that indicate which locations are participating in the sale. As an alternative to the use of volunteers, you could simply place the maps in flyer distribution boxes that are similar to those used by real estate firms.

- Use a consistent roadside decoration, such as balloons, bright streamers, flags, etc., to mark the individual locations participating in the sale. This makes it easier for shoppers to correlate the maps with the actual sale locations. It also makes it easier for those who did not get a map to still identify the sale locations.

- Distribute a supply of maps to each participating location so that any shoppers who failed to receive one earlier can get one.
- Use "More This Way" arrow signs at various inter-sections to help direct and encourage shoppers to continue to seek out all the various sale locations.

In the end, no matter how you arrange your signs, you will want to periodically check on them during the sale. Unfortunately, you will occasionally find people who, for various reasons, will remove or change your signs.

Out of respect for your neighborhood, as soon as your sale is over you should promptly remove all of your signs. In fact, depending on the degree of difficulty, some people may choose to put up their signs each morning and take them down each evening. If your sale is scheduled to last for more than one day and you elect to keep your signs up for the entire period, you must be sure to put the dates and hours that the sale will take place on all signs; otherwise, you will have shoppers showing up too early or too late looking for your sale.

# CHAPTER NINE

# PRICING ITEMS AND RECORDING SALES

There is no exact science for pricing the items you choose to include in your sale. However, for most items the ultimate price should reflect how quickly you wish to sell them or how concerned you are about still having them at the end of the sale.

Significant pricing guidelines, ideas, and things to remember are:

- Price to Sell—The reason you are having a garage sale is to dispose of items that you no longer want or find useful and earn a few dollars in the process. From the very start of your sale, attractively pricing your sale items will help you achieve both ends.

- Base Prices—If you are at a loss for how to price an item, consider what you would be willing to pay for it if you were a potential buyer. Remember, potential buyers will not be interested in paying even discount-store prices for the items that you have used or had in your possession for some time. Once you have arrived at a base price, consider adding an amount such as 15 percent or 20 percent to the price to give you bargaining room.

- Price Gaps—Count on the fact that even if you have priced your sale items attractively, there may still be gaps between what you are asking and what you are ultimately offered. Many shoppers who go to these sales have a strong desire to negotiate prices. These people know that the primary reason you are having a sale is to dispose of items and that sometimes price is a secondary consideration. Also, most like to believe that they are good bargainers and will feel better about their purchases if they can negotiate even a small discount off the initial asking price. As suggested above, adding an additional 15 percent to 20 percent to your base prices should make bargaining easier.

- Bottom-Line Prices—Although you might be eager to sell all the items you are offering, for the most valuable items, you should have some bottom-line figures below which you will not be willing to negotiate. Below these limits your instincts will probably tell you that giving valuable items to charity and perhaps taking a tax deduction will be a better deal.

- Firm Prices—There may be a few items that from the very beginning you decide to price at amounts that are nonnegotiable. If so, you should put a sign on each of these items declaring that "The marked price on this item is firm." Hopefully, you will not have many of these items, because firm prices tend to reduce the success of your sale.

- Price All Items—Mark your initially selected price on each item or bundle of items. It will be helpful if you use a light-colored tape and a dark marker to label the prices. Alternatively, you may choose to use different-colored labels as price indicators, e.g., red labels on $1.00 items, green labels on $5.00 items, etc. If you use a colored-label pricing system, clearly display a sign that shows the price each color represents. It is not a good idea to try to group the items by price and apply no labels. Unfortunately, unless there are only a few sale items, the "grouping" approach can lead to price identity confusion when buyers are ready to pay for their purchases. If involved in a multi-family sale, you should certainly consider using different-colored labels for the items from each family. Lastly, if you do not want to create your own price labels, you can buy pre-printed pricing stickers in multiple colors at some discount and office-supply stores.

- Consider Early Price Reductions—If there is absolutely no interest in some of your items in the early hours and days of your sale, consider reducing the initial prices. Do not wait until the end of your sale to make this decision. Reducing prices at your sale's end when the number of shoppers starts to decrease may not do much to help increase sales. Again, your intent is to dispose of items, not hold on to them.

Significant sales recording ideas and other recommendations primarily for multi-family sales are:

- Keeping Track—If you are having a single-family, community, estate, charity, or rummage sale you won't be too concerned about keeping track of your sales. However, if you are having a multi-family sale, being able to keep track of sales on a by-family basis is a must. As previously mentioned, a very effective way of beginning to deal with such is to utilize different-colored labels for each family. However, in addition to the different-colored labels, you will ultimately need some system for keeping track of the price received for each item on a by-family basis.

- Establishing a Central Pay Point—It would be very confusing and time-consuming if you required your buyers to seek out different family representatives for each of the various items they wished to purchase. A major step toward overcoming this issue as well as the tracking issue is to use designated volunteers to collect all monies and record all of the sales at a central pay point. Establishing a central pay-point will be easy; however, recording the sales on a by-family basis will require additional effort.

- Recording Approaches—A solution for dealing with the recording issue is to use ledger paper or a plain piece of paper with columns representing each family and their respective price-label color. You could also use a laptop computer and a spreadsheet program for this task. When buyers present their selected items for purchase, the designated volunteers can not only total the cost, collect the entire amount and put all the money in a common cash fund, but they can also take steps to verify that the per-family dollar distribution is correctly recorded on a ledger or spreadsheet. Sometimes it is helpful to appoint one of the designated volunteers to serve as the official record keeper. When this is done, the dollar distribution per family by color and price is simply announced to the record keeper for proper recording, e.g., $5 for the blue family, $7 for the red family, etc. As an alternative, the volunteers collecting the money could remove the colored price sticker from each item, correct it for any negotiated price change, and simply hand it to the record keeper for recording. At the end of the sale, you can then distribute the appropriate amount of money from the common cash fund to each family based on the total dollar amount of their sales as shown on the record keeper's sales record.

- Negotiating Prices—Another important issue that impacts most multi-family sales is that of price negotiation. If you have a centralized pay point as recommended above, with whom does the potential buyer negotiate when he or she wishes to buy items from more than one family? Again, it can be very confusing and unproductive to have potential buyers going back and forth to locate a family representative who can negotiate each item's price. The solution is for each family to agree prior to the beginning of the sale to allow the volunteers collecting the money an overall amount of negotiation latitude, such as 20 percent, on any item. This approach will usually work for the majority of sale situations. However, a family representative should be on site or available by phone so that he or she can be consulted if a potential buyer ultimately insists on a greater reduction and it appears reasonable.

# CHAPTER TEN

# DISPLAYING SALE ITEMS

When organizing your sale, it is not necessary to spend money to create attractive displays for sale items. You can put together effective displays from items that you already have or that you can borrow from friends or relatives.

The objectives of sale displays are twofold: (1) present items in a clean, well-lit, and safe environment and (2) display them so that the best aspects of each item are clearly visible.

The following are a number of readily available things that you can use to create your displays:

- Card Tables or Folding Tables—Arrange sale items on one or more card or folding tables.

- Ladders—Secure a strong rod or broomstick between two open stepladders to create a rack for displaying clothes.

- Packing Crates or Packing Boxes—Cover packing crates or strong boxes with plain paper, a solid-colored bed sheet, a large table cloth, or other similar material to create useful counters.

- Shelving—Make shelves by placing boards on bricks, concrete blocks, or upside down trash cans to provide considerable display space. (If you use trash cans, be sure that they are clean and do not give off any offensive odors.)

- Saw Horses—Place boards or used doors between two or more saw horses to create very long display tables

- Garage Doors—Hang clothes or other somewhat light items on the outer edges of your fully opened garage doors.

- Garage Walls—Put up temporary nails or hangers on your garage walls to add display space.

- In-House Tables—Borrow the kitchen table or other casual tables from inside the house and use them for additional displays.

- Tarpaulins—Lay down a tarpaulin or some other clean material to protect and highlight very heavy items or items that are going to be displayed on the ground.

- Driveway—Line up large or cumbersome items on your driveway or sidewalk in a graduated fashion, beginning with the smaller items closest to the street and taller or larger items further up for a sufficiently attractive and visible display.

- Photos—If one or more sale items are too cumbersome to move outside, take pictures of each item, and mount the pictures on poster board with detailed descriptions and asking prices. Then prominently display the poster board on an easel, wall, etc. Serious buyers who are interested will usually ask to see the items and at that time they can be escorted into your residence to examine them.

- Open House—If due to circumstances almost everything in your residence is for sale, it might be easier to set up your displays on a room-to-room basis and allow shoppers to walk through all rooms that contain your displays. However, be sure to close or tape off any rooms that contain non-sale items.

Again, it is crucial that the areas in which you set up your displays—garage, yard, driveway, or sidewalk—be safe, clean, well lit, odor free, and easily accessible. And, to the extent possible, you should display all sale items at least at table height. Having to get down and dig through piles of items on the ground may be a physical impossibility for some shoppers.

When displaying your items, don't forget to attempt to group them by nature, function, or type. Shoppers who are interested in tools might not be interested in kitchen items.

Additionally, when arranging the layout of your display tables, make sure that the walkway between them is wide enough for people to pass and to be able to spend time looking at continuous rows of items on either side. You want shoppers to be encouraged by your layout to circulate around all of your displays before leaving. Having a narrow walkway with scattered displays and items only on one side is poor use of display space and may tend to discourage your shoppers from looking at everything.

After you have set up your displays examine the surrounding area for distractions. You may have a vintage motorcycle or large collection of shop tools in the same area that are not for sale. If this is your situation and you do not want to move them, you should at least cover them up. If you can't completely hide these non-sale items, consider roping off the area in which they are located and putting a sign on the rope that indicates that the items in the area are not for sale.

Keep in mind that as you sell your items there will be gaps in your displays. When this begins to happen, quickly consolidate and rearrange your displays to close these gaps and, if necessary, change your walkway. As the sale continues, you do not want newly arriving shoppers to get the impression that most of the items are gone and your sale is about over.

Remember that most buyers at these sales are impulse buyers. They are attracted to something that you have on display, think it might be of use to them, and agree to purchase it. This makes your displays very important. Unfortunately, many of these sales are not very successful simply because of poor displays. You can vastly improve your sales by having efficient and attractive displays!

# CHAPTER ELEVEN

# A PRESALE

No matter how hard you try to minimize the impacts some of your neighbors will be affected by such things as traffic congestion, noise, and trespassers on their lawns during your sale.

One of the ways to help compensate them for any inconvenience is to invite your immediate neighbors to a private presale the evening before it officially begins. You might even consider having light refreshments for those who attend and making it celebratory event. This will give your neighbors first choice of any items that they might wish to purchase. Plus, it will tend to buy a little goodwill, which could be very useful during and after the sale.

# CHAPTER TWELVE

# CONDUCT DURING THE SALE

How you greet and treat your shoppers will have a lot to do with how comfortable they will be when they come to your sale; moreover, their degree of comfort will have much to do with how long they spend looking at your sale items.

You should greet shoppers with a pleasant smile and a warm welcome. When speaking to them, look directly at them and don't forget to encourage them to browse through your sale items. You should also encourage them to ask questions, test items of interest, and pick up the boxes or plastic bags you have available for carrying the things that they are accumulating. Additionally, while they shop you should provide them with a secure place to set aside larger items that they wish to purchase so that others will know that these items are no longer for sale.

When shoppers ask questions about any item, you should respond promptly and truthfully. However, you should avoid making emotional remarks regarding the item's prior use, such as "The phone works perfectly and was last used by my dying farther when he made his final 911 call!"

Remember that if the shoppers who come to your sales are comfortable and have a good experience, they are more likely to keep coming back every time you have a sale.

Lastly, although it is not a very common practice and is certainly not required for a successful sale, you might consider offering those who attend a small cup of coffee and/or cookies. Another, and perhaps more financially rewarding version of this approach, is to offer a variety of non-alcoholic beverages for a small charge. (This is a great job for younger family members who would like to set up a beverage stand and earn a little money for themselves or charity.) In any case, those who offer refreshments tend to believe that doing so encourages shoppers to spend more time looking at their sale items, which they hope will equate to increased sales.

# CHAPTER THIRTEEN

# HANDLING AWKWARD SITUATIONS

During your sale awkward situations such as the following might occur:

- Two people want the same item and both are emphatic that they were the first to choose the item.

- Someone is sure that you charged them too much for a given item, because the item was found among lower-priced items or was not clearly marked.

- A potential buyer insists that an item you are offering as an antique is not one and thus is not very valuable.

- In the payment process someone believes that that he or she was shortchanged and is due back more money.

- Someone wants an assurance that if the item purchased does not work, a return and refund is possible.

- A person wants to buy the item, but the final price is more than the cash that he or she has immediately available.

- Someone wants a given item but is only able to offer a check as payment.

- You observe someone shoplifting.

Advanced thinking about how best to handle these kinds of situations will do a lot to make your sale less stressful and more enjoyable.

## People Who Want the Same Item

When two people want and believe they are entitled to the same item, you could handle it one of two possible ways: (1) allow the two to bid, with the item going to the highest bidder, or (2) ask a stranger, not you, to pick a number and the potential buyer whose guess is closest gets the item. You can sometimes soften the blow for the one who was not successful in getting the desired item by giving that person a special discount on any remaining items that he or she wishes to purchase.

## Conflict over Price

People who are adamant about having been charged too much because an item was located with lesser-cost items or has been poorly marked are always difficult to deal with. Generally, if you allowed them to carry on, they will consume your time and distract other shoppers or potential buyers. Keeping in mind that the overall purpose of your sale is to rid yourself of unwanted items, attempt to deal with the situation quickly. One way to handle it is to state that you believe there has been a mistake, that the true price is a given amount, and that you are willing to deep discount the price. If this does not appease the person, then your choices are to either permanently remove it from your sale or take the price offered, regardless of how low it might be.

## Antique Verification

If you believe a particular item that you wish to offer for sale might be an antique and has some significant value, you should have the item appraised before the sale and be prepared to furnish a copy of the appraisal to anyone who is interested in buying it. Knowing the appraised value will be helpful to all parties, particularly during the sale negotiation process.

## Shortchanged Situations

When it comes to money, everyone is sensitive to some extent. The best way to assure that there is no confusion regarding correct change is to always place the amount the buyer has given you to one side and give him or her change from your own money first. Once the buyer is satisfied, then you can put his or her money with yours.

## Return Policy

You should remind all buyers of electrical or mechanical items that all sales are "final as is" and there will be no exceptions. Some electrical or mechanical items may operate well and some may not. If you know of any significant problems with such items, you should disclose them by attaching a descriptive note. Additionally, buyers of any electrical or mechanical items should be encouraged to test them before making their purchases. To facilitate testing you should have a working extension cord available for them to plug in electrical items and batteries for them "To Borrow" to test battery-powered items. Due to the nature of garage sales it is not practical to guarantee the operation of any item. To reinforce this position, you might find it helpful to post a notice to this effect.

# Not Enough Money

There will be occasions when someone wants to purchase an item but did not bring enough money to cover the cost. In such a case, you can always request a deposit and agree to hold the item until the potential buyer can return with the remaining money. And when you take a deposit, don't forget to give a receipt. Also, as part of this arrangement, you should seek an agreement on a "same-day" time limit for the potential buyer's return. If the time limit passes and he or she has not returned, put the item back on sale and set aside the deposit money to give back whenever he or she eventually returns. Otherwise, the person could knock on your door well after the sale is over, declare that the item is no longer wanted, and request a return of the deposit leaving you with the unwanted item and no opportunity to resell it.

# Acceptance of Checks

Accepting checks for garage sale items is risky. For this reason, almost all such sales are conducted on a "cash only" basis. If the buyer does not have sufficient cash at the time he or she wishes to purchase an item, you can use the above cash-deposit approach, or if you think you know the person well enough, you can take a chance on a check. If you do decide to take a check, it would be wise to cash the check at the bank on which it was drawn the next business day. This action will give you some slight protection against insufficient funds.

## Shoplifting

Believe it or not there are cases of shoplifting during garage sales. If you observe someone shoplifting, your best recourse is to politely ask if you can hold the item for the person until he or she has finished looking at everything and is ready to checkout. This will make it clear to the shoplifter that you know what has happened. However, if the shoplifter insists that he or she does not have such an item, your best recourse is simply to withdraw and continue to watch the person very carefully. Remember, you are not the police, and even if you called them, it is unlikely that they would respond quickly to a shoplifting incident during your sale. When it comes to shoplifting, your best defense is to have enough helpers so that you can station them throughout the sale area. This will help make sure that all shoppers will be well served and also reasonably watched. This is particularly the case when you are selling small items and perhaps items of some value. Another shoplifting protective approach involves the placing of valuable items in or under glass or plastic cases, accessible only upon on request.

As the organizer of the sale, the above text is primarily for your benefit. However it is also useful for those who will be helping you; therefore, before the sale begins, you may want to take a few minutes with your helpers to review some of these awkward situations and how you wish to handle them.

# CHAPTER FOURTEEN

# AFTER THE SALE

There are seven things that you will need to do after your sale is over. They are as follows:

- Decide what to do with the unsold items.
- Take down and/or collect all directional signs.
- Return any borrowed display support material.
- Thank and reward the volunteers who helped.
- Thank your neighbors.
- Deposit the sale money.
- Begin to make plans for your next sale.

## Unsold Items

Regardless of your best efforts, when your sale is over there will no doubt be some unsold items. What do you do with these items?

Give them to charity. This could serve four useful purposes: (1) it will negate your need to continue to handle and store things that you have already committed to part with; (2) it could provide others with items that will be useful to them; (3) it will redistribute and recycle the items, and (4) it could provide you with a tax deduction for your donation.

## Take Down and/or Collect Signs

Promptly remove all directional and informational signs, posters, etc. relating to your sale. This is very important. Just imagine what your neighborhood or community would look like if everyone who put up signs ignored their responsibility to remove them when they were no longer applicable.

## Return Borrowed Materials

As with signs, be prompt in returning any borrowed materials that were used to help stage your sale. Prompt return of such material this time should make it easier for you to borrow again for your next sale.

## Thank Volunteers

Unless you have a very small sale, you will most likely have pressed into service family members, friends, and/or neighbors to help you. They will no doubt have contributed their time to help make your sale successful and thus will deserve your thanks and, perhaps, some reward for their work. The reward does not have to be monetary. It can be something such as a barbecue meal, pizza dinner, snack party, etc.

## Thank Neighbors

Call or stop by to thank your neighbors, who were not involved with your sale, for putting up with any inconvenience that the sale might have caused them. Such consideration will go a long way toward securing their cooperation when you decide to have another sale.

## Deposit Money

Hopefully your sale has been financially successful. If so, be sure to put the money in a safe place, preferably in the bank.

Obviously your sale was well publicized in your community, and since these sales are well-known for their cash-based business, there may be those who would be tempted to rob you. In today's society, due to drugs or other pressures, robberies have taken place even for very small amounts of money, particularly where nontraceable cash is involved.

## The Next Sale

While the sale's event is fresh in your mind, it is a good time to think about what you would do differently next time you organize another sale. Space has been provided in the back of this book to record these thoughts so that they will be easily accessible at a later time.

Additionally, you should consider designating a particular space in your house as a place to accumulate, over time, the items that you wish to include in future sales. Such action will eliminate the need for any last-minute searches to locate your next sale's items.

# CHAPTER FIFTEEN

# CELEBRATE YOUR SUCCESS

If, after your sale is over, you have sold most of what you have offered, had fun, and collected some money for your effort, you have had a successful sale. Congratulations!

Hopefully the advice you found in this book made a significant contribution to the success that you just experienced.

Too often people who take action and achieve what they set out to accomplish simply move from one accomplishment to another without taking time to celebrate their successes. Don't let this happen to you!

After your successful sale, reward yourself. You have done well. Give yourself a gift, a day off, or do something that you personally have wanted to do for some time but have been putting off.

Lastly, continue to keep this book handy, use it as a reference book, and read it again prior to your next sale. The interesting thing about how-to books is that each time you read them you continue to learn more and become more skilled and successful at what you are doing.

William Hazlitt once said, "A strong passion for any object will ensure success, for the desire of the end will point out the means." This is certainly true for garage sales.

Best wishes for many future successful sales!

# ORGANIZATIONAL NOTES
# FOR FUTURE SALES

_____

_____

_____

_____

_____

_____

_____

_____

_____

_____

_____

_____

_____

_____

# ADDENDUM

## BUYERS' GUIDE

One more thing! Since most garage-sale organizers are or will become garage-sale buyers before finally concluding this book, it seems appropriate to offer the following basic guidelines for negotiating and buying sale items:

- Hold on to the Item—When you find something that you think you might like to buy hold on to it or have the seller set it aside for you. Otherwise, while you are looking at other items someone else may buy it. If, before you pay for it, you decide you do not want the item, simply return it to the seller.

- Carefully Examine the Item—Make sure that the item you are thinking about purchasing operates properly and/or is in an acceptable condition. If electricity or batteries power the item, ask to test it. Remember, all garage-sale sales are final!

- Don't Be Greedy—If the initial sale price is already very attractive or the item is not expensive, don't be greedy and try to insist on a price reduction. Unfortunately, for the sake of ego or some other driving force, there are those who will attempt to seek a lower price even on a fifty-cent item. Think how you would like to be treated if you were selling the item.

- Explore the Negotiating Option—If the price is a lot more than you are willing to pay or can afford, but you still want the item, don't be afraid to inquire if the initial price is open to negotiation. If the answer is an absolute no, thank the seller, and forget the purchase. However, if there is any indication that the seller might be willing to consider a lower price, begin to negotiate. When attempting to negotiate a lower price, adhering to the following guidelines should be helpful:

  ✓ Negotiate Only with the Seller—Avoid discussing any offer you might consider making with assistants or helpers.

  ✓ Be Personable—People who exhibit an arrogant or hard-nose attitude and immediately insist on a lower price will not impress the seller or give him or her any encouragement to reduce the price. Plus, it is inconsiderate to use an ultimatum as a negotiating strategy.

✓ Act Confident—Look the seller in the eye, and do not appear as if you are embarrassed about any offer you might choose to make.

✓ Don't Overnegotiate—Some people feel that they need to point out everything they can find wrong with the item in order to get the price down. They even try to convince the seller that if he or she does not sell it to them at their price, it may never sell. They forget that this is the seller's property, and when first pricing it, the seller has usually considered all of its flaws and salability.

✓ Stay Calm—Remain calm even if the seller appears agitated by your efforts to negotiate or makes a counteroffer.

✓ Be Fair and Reasonable—Even after making what is considered to be a good offer, relative to the initial asking price, be open to a counteroffer by the seller. In many cases it may be possible to settle on a price somewhere in the middle.

✓ Know Your Limits—If an item is only worth so much to you and the price cannot be reduced enough to truly justify its purchase, be willing to politely walk away without buying it. It should be noted that when some sellers see that a potential buyer's price limit has finally been reached, a willingness to make a last-minute concession could occur. However, never count on this as a successful negotiating strategy.

✓ End on a Courteous Note—Whether you get the lower price that you are seeking, settle on a compromise price in the middle, or pay the original asking price, express your appreciation to the seller for taking the time to consider your offer or offers.

For the garage-sale shopper, the ultimate question will always be "To buy or not to buy?" Only the shopper can make this decision and initiate the appropriate steps to complete a purchase. If you are the seller, do your best to make the items that you are offering for sale as attractive as possible. If you are a buyer, do your best to treat the seller with the same degree of respect that you would appreciate as a seller.

# NEVER FORGET

*Nothing is ever accomplished without effort. Conducting a well-organized and successful garage sale will only be as rewarding and satisfying as you make it!*

Jon Fulghum

# NOTE FROM THE AUTHOR

Sometimes readers wish to get in touch with the authors of the books that they read. If you would like to contact me regarding this book and you have Internet access, I would suggest that you consider going to my web site and leaving me an e-mail message. My web site address is: jonfulghum.com

When attempting to contact me, please keep the following in mind:

- ❑ If you decide to write me a letter, and mail it to my publisher, there is a good chance that it will become the sad victim of the paperwork shuffle that takes place between publisher and author. Bottom line, personal letters are rarely responded to.

- ❑ If you e-mail me a message via my web site, my response time may not be quick, but overall it is good.

- ❑ If you do elect to contact me by e-mail, please do not forward me attachments, send me ideas for other books, nor add me to any mailing lists. Such information is usually deleted without any response.

- ❑ If you would like to inquire about speaking arrangements, book signing event scheduling, or other appearances you can also do so by visiting my web site.

I appreciate your willingness to purchase and read my book. Without you, its continued publication and the publication of future books would not be possible.

978-0-595-41744-5
0-595-41744-2

CPSIA information can be obtained at www.ICGtesting.com
227780LV00001B/190-192/A